USE YOUR NOODLE!

RECIPES FOR RAMEN, SOBA, UDON AND OTHER NOODLES

This edition published by Parragon Books Ltd in 2014
LOVE FOOD is an imprint of Parragon Books Ltd

Parragon Books Ltd
Chartist House
15–17 Trim Street
Bath BA1 1HA, UK
www.parragon.com/lovefood

ISBN 978-1-4723-6451-7

Printed in China

Project managed by Kerry Starr
New recipes written by Robin Donovan
New photography by Mike Cooper
New home economy by Lincoln Jefferson
Introduction and incidental text written by Rachel Carter
New internal illustrations by Nicola O'Byrne
Production Controller: Joe Xavier

Notes for the Reader

This book uses both metric and imperial measurements. Follow the same units of measurement throughout; do not mix metric and imperial. All spoon measurements are level: teaspoons are assumed to be 5 ml, and tablespoons are assumed to be 15 ml. Unless otherwise stated, milk is assumed to be full fat, eggs and individual vegetables are medium, and pepper is freshly ground black pepper. Unless otherwise stated, all root vegetables should be peeled prior to using.

Garnishes, decorations and serving suggestions are all optional and not necessarily included in the recipe ingredients or method. The times given are an approximate guide only. Preparation times differ according to the techniques used by different people and the cooking times may also vary from those given. Optional ingredients, variations or serving suggestions have not been included in the time calculations.

USE YOUR
NOODLE!

CONTENTS

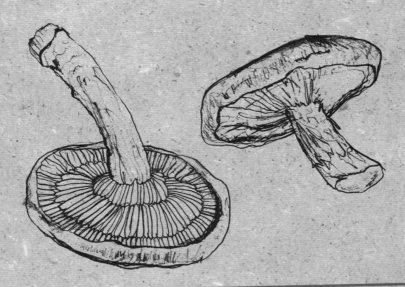

SOBA SO GOOD...

THE HISTORY OF THE NOODLE

noodle: a very long thin strip of pasta or similar flour paste, eaten with a sauce or in a soup

origin: late 18th century from the German term nudel

- - - - - - - - - - - - - - - -

The exact origin of noodles seems to be clouded in mystery and it has been the subject of much debate. Indeed whole books have been devoted to the subject of this much loved food which is essentially a starch based dough, sold in a variety of shapes and thicknesses, some sold in coils and others in bundles.

Whether Marco Polo the Italian Merchant traveller brought noodles from China to Italy via the Silk Road is unproven, but their evolution is an interesting one.

What seems certain is that the ancestor to the noodle was not called a 'noodle'. In the Eastern Han Dynasty 'cake' is the original term associated with anything made with flour and water, and initially it was not formed into the string-like pieces that we think of as noodles.

In the 3rd century A.D. a Chinese dictionary refers to them as 'mian pian' or little pieces of bread dough, whilst in the 5th century A.D. in the Jerusalem Talmud there are references to a food resembling a noodle in shape made from semolina called 'itrium'.

6

In 2002 archaeologists made a fascinating discovery at the Lajia excavations near the Yellow River in North West China. The oldest known noodles were found and using carbon dating, placed at around 4,000 years old. They were preserved in an overturned sealed bowl buried under 3 metres of sediment. The yellow noodles were long and thin and thought to be made by hand stretching the dough, showing a high level of culinary sophistication. Interestingly they were found to be derived from two types of millet: foxtail and broomcorn both of which were indigenous to China and widely cultivated around 7,000 years ago.

The earliest mention of noodles dates back to a book in China's Eastern Han Dynasty between A.D. 25 and 200, when they were often made from wheat dough. It's thought they were a staple in the diets of many in that period.

Whilst the Arabs, Chinese and Italians all lay claim to noodles, it seems certain that the Italians should be credited with spreading their popularity throughout the world.

Instant noodles were first marketed in Japan in 1958, when it was discovered that drying fresh noodles and then flash frying them prolonged their shelf life.

9

A BIRD IN THE HAND

TURKEY MISO SOUP

This comforting soup, enriched with miso paste, is just the thing to warm you up on a damp winter's day.

SERVES: 4   **PREP TIME: 5 MINS**   **COOK TIME: 25 MINS**

INGREDIENTS

225 g/8 oz fresh udon noodles

1 tbsp vegetable oil

1 small leek, white and light green parts halved lengthways and thinly sliced

2.4 litres/4 pints turkey stock

3 carrots, sliced

1 tsp white pepper

225 g/8 oz sugar snap peas, halved

280 g/10 oz cooked turkey meat, shredded or chopped

4 tbsp white miso paste

1. Cook the noodles according to the packet instructions.

2. Heat the oil in a medium-sized saucepan over a medium–high heat. Add the leek and cook, stirring frequently, for 3 minutes, or until it begins to soften. Add the stock, carrots and pepper and bring to the boil. Reduce the heat to low and simmer for 15 minutes, or until the carrots are just tender.

3. Add the sugar snap peas, turkey and cooked noodles and simmer for 2–3 minutes until heated through. Stir in the miso paste until it is dissolved. Taste and adjust the seasoning if necessary.

4. Transfer the soup to warmed bowls and serve immediately.

HERO TIPS

This soup is great to have in the freezer so that you can heat up a bowl whenever you like. It's best to cook and add the noodles just before serving.

CHICKEN NOODLE SOUP

SERVES: 4-6   **PREP TIME: 15 MINS**   **COOK TIME: 35 MINS**

INGREDIENTS

2 boneless, skinless
chicken breasts

2 litres/3½ pints water

1 onion, with skin left on,
cut in half

1 large garlic clove,
cut in half

1-cm/½-inch piece fresh
ginger, peeled and sliced

4 black peppercorns,
lightly crushed

4 cloves

2 star anise

1 celery stick, chopped

100 g/3½ oz baby corn cobs,
sliced

2 spring onions,
finely shredded

115 g/4 oz dried rice
vermicelli noodles

1 carrot, peeled and coarsely
grated

salt and pepper

1. Put the chicken breasts and water into a saucepan and bring to the boil. Reduce the heat and simmer, skimming the surface until no more foam rises.

2. Add the onion, garlic, ginger, peppercorns, cloves, star anise and a pinch of salt.

3. Continue to simmer for 20 minutes, or until the chicken is no longer pink when cut into.

4. Strain the chicken, reserving about 1.2 litres/2 pints stock, but discarding any flavouring solids. Return the reserved stock to the rinsed out pan and add the celery, baby corn cobs and spring onions.

5. Bring the stock to the boil and boil until the baby corn cobs are almost tender, then add the noodles and continue boiling for 2 minutes.

6. Meanwhile, chop the chicken, add to the pan with the grated carrot and continue cooking for about 1 minute, until the chicken is re-heated and the noodles are soft. Season to taste with salt and pepper.

7. Transfer the soup to warmed bowls and serve immediately.

ROASTED DUCK SOUP WITH MUSHROOMS & EGGS

SERVES: 4   **PREP TIME: 10 MINS, PLUS SOAKING**   **COOK TIME: 50 MINS**

INGREDIENTS

15 g/½ oz dried shiitake mushrooms

1.7 litres/3 pints chicken or duck stock

4 tbsp Chinese rice wine, dry sherry or dry white wine

10-cm/4-inch piece fresh ginger, peeled and sliced

2 tbsp rice vinegar

2 tbsp soy sauce

2 tsp sesame oil

1 cinnamon stick

1 star anise pod

1 tsp white pepper

1 tsp salt

225 g/8 oz roast duck meat (preferably dark meat), shredded

175 g/6 oz fresh shiitake mushrooms, sliced

175 g/6 oz dried ramen noodles (flavouring sachet discarded, if included)

4 spring onions, sliced diagonally into 2.5-cm/1-inch pieces

4 eggs

chilli oil, to garnish

1. Soak the dried mushrooms in hot water for 30 minutes. Drain, reserving the liquid, and slice.

2. Combine the stock, wine, mushroom soaking liquid, ginger, vinegar, soy sauce, sesame oil, cinnamon stick, star anise, pepper and salt in a large saucepan. Bring to a simmer, then reduce the heat to low and simmer for 20 minutes. Strain the stock and discard the ginger slices. Return the stock, star anise and cinnamon stick to the pot. Bring back to a simmer and add the duck meat, the reserved soaked dried mushrooms and the fresh mushrooms. Simmer for a further 20 minutes, or until the mushrooms are tender. Remove the cinnamon stick and star anise, increase the heat and bring the soup back to the boil.

3. Add the noodles and cook, breaking them up with a spoon as needed, for about 3 minutes, or until tender. Stir in the spring onions.

4. To cook the eggs, half-fill a medium-sized saucepan with water and bring to the boil over a high heat. Reduce the heat to low and carefully crack the eggs into the water. Cook for 4 minutes.

5. Ladle the soup into warmed bowls and top each with an egg. Garnish with a few drops of chilli oil and serve immediately.

CHINESE CHICKEN SALAD

SERVES: 4　　　　**PREP TIME: 20 MINS**　　　　**COOK TIME: 10 MINS**

INGREDIENTS

3 boneless, skinless chicken
breasts, weighing 450 g/
1 lb in total, cut into
bite-sized pieces

2 tsp soy sauce

¼ tsp freshly ground
white pepper

2 tbsp groundnut oil,
plus extra for deep-frying

50 g/1¾ oz thin rice noodles

½ head Chinese leaves,
thinly sliced diagonally

3 spring onions, green parts
included, sliced diagonally

40 g/1½ oz almonds with skin,
sliced lengthways

sesame seeds, to garnish
(optional)

DRESSING

5 tbsp olive oil

3 tbsp rice vinegar

3 tbsp soy sauce

a few drops sesame oil

salt and pepper

1. Sprinkle the chicken with the soy sauce and white pepper. To make the dressing, whisk the ingredients together in a bowl until well blended.

2. Heat a wok over a high heat, then add the groundnut oil. Stir-fry the chicken for 4–5 minutes until brown. Drain on kitchen paper and allow to cool. Wipe out the wok.

3. Pour enough groundnut oil for deep-frying into the wok. Heat to 180–190°C/350–375°F or until a cube of bread browns in 30 seconds, then fry a few noodles at a time until puffed up and crisp. Remove and drain on kitchen paper.

4. Arrange the Chinese leaves in a shallow serving dish. Place the noodles in a pile on top of the leaves on one side of the dish. Arrange the chicken, spring onions and almonds in the remaining space. Whisk the dressing again and pour over the salad. Garnish with the sesame seeds, if using. Serve immediately.

DUCK & CRISPY RAMEN NOODLE SALAD

SERVES: 4   **PREP TIME: 20 MINS**   **COOK TIME: 15 MINS**

INGREDIENTS

85 g/3 oz dried ramen noodles (flavouring sachet discarded, if included)

2 duck breasts halves, about 175 g/6 oz each

225 ml/8 fl oz groundnut oil

salt and pepper

2 tbsp sliced toasted almonds, to garnish

DRESSING

juice of 1 lime

2 tbsp white miso paste

1 tbsp reduced-salt soy sauce

1 tbsp unseasoned rice vinegar

1 tsp grated fresh ginger

4 tbsp vegetable oil

1 tsp sesame oil

SALAD

1 Little Gem lettuce, torn into bite-sized pieces

4 clementines, peeled and sectioned

1 red jalapeño chilli, deseeded and finely diced

1 avocado, diced

2 tbsp sliced toasted almonds

1. Preheat the oven to 200°C/400°F/Gas Mark 6. Line a plate with kitchen paper.

2. Cook the noodles according to the packet instructions. Drain and arrange in small clumps on the prepared plate and set aside to dry.

3. To cook the duck, heat a large ovenproof frying pan over a medium heat. Pat the duck breasts dry and season with salt and pepper. Using a very sharp knife, score the skin, making 4–6 slashes across the top of each breast, being careful not to cut into the meat. When the pan is hot, add the duck breasts, skin-side down, and cook for 5–6 minutes, or until most of the fat is rendered and the skin is brown and crisp. Turn and cook for 2 minutes on the other side, until just beginning to brown. Turn the breasts again and place the pan in the preheated oven. Roast for 7–9 minutes, or until a meat thermometer registers 55°C/130°F when inserted into the thickest part of the meat. Remove from the oven and leave to rest for at least 5 minutes before slicing. Slice across the grain into 5-mm/ ¼-inch thick slices.

4. To make the crispy noodles, line a plate with kitchen paper. Put the oil in a small saucepan and heat over a high heat until just beginning to smoke. Using tongs, add the noodles, one clump at a time, and cook for about 20 seconds, until golden brown. Turn and cook on the other side for a further 15–20 seconds until golden brown. Transfer to the prepared plate to drain.

5. To make the dressing, whisk together the first 5 ingredients in a small bowl. Add the vegetable oil and sesame oil and whisk until combined and emulsified.

6. To assemble, toss together the salad ingredients in a large bowl. Drizzle 4 tablespoons of the dressing over the salad and toss to coat. Divide the salad between plates and top each with several slices of duck, sprinkle with the almonds and drizzle over a little more dressing. Add the noodles and serve immediately.

THAI CHICKEN & SOBA NOODLE SALAD

SERVES: 4   **PREP TIME: 15 MINS**   **COOK TIME: 10 MINS**

INGREDIENTS

225 g/8 oz dried soba noodles

350 g/12 oz cooked chicken, shredded

1 cucumber, peeled, deseeded and cut into matchsticks

140 g/5 oz cabbage, shredded

1 red pepper, deseeded and cut into matchsticks

3 spring onions, thinly sliced, and 70 g/2½ oz crushed roasted unsalted peanuts, to garnish

DRESSING

juice of 1 lime

1 tbsp Thai fish sauce

1 tbsp soft light brown sugar

2 tbsp smooth peanut butter

1 garlic clove, finely chopped

1–2 small hot red chillies, deseeded and finely chopped

3 tbsp vegetable oil

15 g/½ oz fresh coriander leaves, chopped

15 g/½ oz fresh mint leaves, chopped

1. Cook the noodles according to the packet instructions. Drain and rinse with cold water. Set aside to cool completely.

2. To make the dressing, combine the lime juice, fish sauce, sugar, peanut butter, garlic and chillies in a small bowl and whisk to mix well. Whisk in the oil until well combined and emulsified. Stir in the coriander and mint.

3. Combine the cooked noodles, chicken, cucumber, cabbage and red pepper in a large bowl and toss to combine. Add the dressing and toss again to coat well. Garnish with spring onions and peanuts and serve.

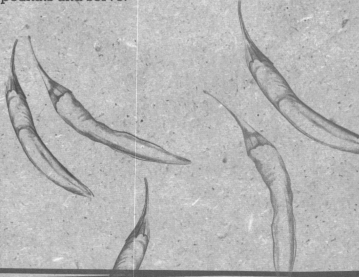

CHICKEN CHOW MEIN

This classic Chinese stir-fry is a familiar take-away favourite. Cooked at home you can add any vegetables that you like, making it not only delicious but adaptable.

SERVES: 4   **PREP TIME: 5-10 MINS**   **COOK TIME: 15 MINS**

INGREDIENTS

250 g/9 oz dried medium Chinese egg noodles

2 tbsp sunflower oil

280 g/10 oz cooked chicken breasts, shredded

1 garlic clove, finely chopped

1 red pepper, thinly sliced

100 g/3½ oz shiitake mushrooms, sliced

6 spring onions, sliced

100 g/3½ oz beansprouts

3 tbsp soy sauce

1 tbsp sesame oil

1. Cook the noodles as per the packet instructions. Drain well and set aside.

2. Heat a wok over a medium heat, then add the oil. Add the shredded chicken, garlic, red pepper, mushrooms, spring onions and beansprouts to the wok and stir-fry for about 5 minutes.

3. Add the noodles to the wok, toss well and stir-fry for a further 5 minutes. Drizzle over the soy sauce and sesame oil and toss until thoroughly combined. Transfer to warmed bowls and serve immediately.

WOK ON!
(HOW TO COOK, SERVE & EAT NOODLES)

It's worth clarifying that in general wheat based noodles are different from pasta in that they are made with a much softer variety of wheat. The durum wheat used in pasta gives a much firmer end product than silky noodles with their characteristic soft texture which also cook much quicker than pasta.

Naturally the type of noodle you choose determines how you cook and eat them, and it's always best to refer to the cooking instructions given on the packaging.

Noodle dough tends to have plenty of salt already added to help develop the softer protein and help bind the dough. This helps to preserve the noodles once dried. Therefore there is no need to add salt to the cooking water. The other main difference is that pasta is extruded (rather like squeezing toothpaste from a tube) whereas noodle dough is rolled and then cut.

Soaking vs Boiling

To rehydrate dried noodles, they either need to be soaked in boiling water off the heat, then drained or added to a large pan of boiling water. Alternatively they could be cooked in a pan of flavoured broth.

When cooking noodles in advance, e.g. before adding to a stir-fry, the noodles can be cooked and drained then placed in a bowl of ice cold

water to stop the cooking process. Once cool, drain well and toss in a little toasted sesame oil until needed.

To check whether the noodles are cooked, remove a piece of noodle from the pan, cool momentarily and then taste to make sure that it's tender. It's very hard to undercook noodles, but easy to overcook, so bear that in mind if you are going to add the cooked noodles to a stir-fry.

When adding to a wok or pan, heat the wok to a high temperature first, then add the oil. Always lift and toss the noodles rather than trying to stir them in the pan. This will help retain the texture.

Serving Noodles

Noodles are served in a huge number of ways, generally in a hot broth with a dipping sauce or stir-fried with vegetables, meat or fish, or cold in a salad with a dressing.

The etiquette of eating noodles depends on the country in which you are eating. In China it's not seen as acceptable to bite off noodles when eating but a slurping action is the norm. The chopsticks are used to help the noodles into the mouth.

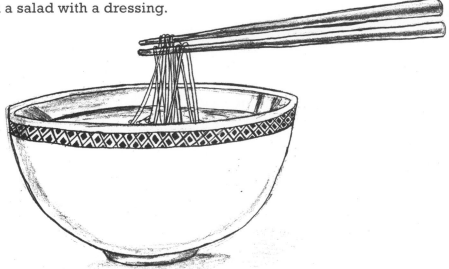

TERIYAKI CHICKEN

SERVES: 4   **PREP TIME: 10 MINS, PLUS MARINATING**   **COOK TIME: 25 MINS**

INGREDIENTS

4 boneless chicken breasts,
about 175 g/6 oz each,
with or without skin

4 tbsp bottled teriyaki sauce,
plus extra if needed

peanut or corn oil,
for brushing

SESAME NOODLES

250 g/9 oz dried thin soba
noodles

1 tbsp toasted sesame oil

2 tbsp sesame seeds, toasted

2 tbsp finely chopped
fresh parsley

salt and pepper

1. Using a sharp knife score each chicken breast diagonally across 3 times. Rub all over with teriyaki sauce. Set aside in the refrigerator to marinate for at least 10 minutes and up to 24 hours.

2. Meanwhile, preheat the grill to high. To make the sesame noodles, cook the noodles according to the packet instructions. Drain well and set aside.

3. Lightly brush the griddle pan with peanut oil. Add the chicken breasts, skin-side up, and brush again with a little extra teriyaki sauce.

4. Griddle the chicken breast, brushing occasionally with extra teriyaki sauce, for 15 minutes, or until tender and the juices run clear when a skewer is inserted into the thickest part of the meat.

5. Meanwhile, heat a wok over a high heat. Add the sesame oil and heat until it shimmers.

6. Add the noodles and stir round to heat through, then stir in the sesame seeds and parsley. Season to taste with salt and pepper.

7. Transfer the chicken breasts to warmed plates and serve immediately with the noodles.

UDON NOODLES WITH HOISIN TURKEY SAUCE

SERVES: 4　　　**PREP TIME: 10 MINS**　　　**COOK TIME: 15 MINS**

INGREDIENTS

450 g/1 lb fresh udon noodles

2 tbsp vegetable oil

2 tbsp finely chopped fresh ginger

2 garlic cloves, finely chopped

1–2 red jalapeño chillies, deseeded and finely chopped

550 g/1 lb 4 oz fresh turkey mince

225 g/8 oz French beans, cut into 2.5-cm/1-inch pieces

70 g/2½ oz water chestnuts, diced

1 tbsp Chinese rice wine, dry sherry or dry white wine

3 spring onions, white and pale green parts thinly sliced, to garnish

SAUCE

125 ml/4 fl oz hoisin sauce

4 tbsp chicken stock or water

2 tbsp sesame oil

2 tbsp rice vinegar

1. Cook the noodles according to the packet instructions. Drain and keep warm.

2. Heat 1 tablespoon of the oil in a large frying pan over a medium–high heat. Add the ginger and cook, stirring, for 1 minute. Add the garlic and chillies and cook, stirring, for a further minute. Add the turkey and cook, stirring and breaking up the meat with a spatula, until the meat is brown all over. Transfer the meat to a bowl.

3. To make the sauce, stir together all of the ingredients in a small bowl and set aside.

4. Heat the remaining oil in a pan. Add the beans and water chestnuts and cook, stirring frequently, for 4 minutes, or until the beans begin to soften. Add the wine and cook, stirring and scraping up any sediment from the base of the pan, for about 1 minute, until the liquid has almost evaporated. Add the reserved turkey to the pan with the hoisin sauce mixture. Cook, stirring occasionally, for a further 4 minutes, or until the sauce is thickened and the beans are tender.

5. Toss the turkey mixture with the noodles, garnish with the spring onions and serve immediately.

THAI GREEN CHICKEN CURRY & UDON NOODLES

SERVES: 4   **PREP TIME: 10 MINS**   **COOK TIME: 15 MINS**

INGREDIENTS

1 tbsp vegetable oil
1 shallot, diced
1–3 tsp Thai green curry paste
425 ml/15 fl oz canned coconut milk
1 tbsp Thai fish sauce
juice of 1 lime
1 tbsp soft light brown sugar
25 g/1 oz fresh basil leaves
25 g/1 oz fresh coriander leaves
450 g/1 lb fresh udon noodles
350 g/12 oz cooked chicken, shredded
3 spring onions, thinly sliced, to garnish

1. Heat the oil in a non-stick frying pan over a medium heat. Add the shallot and cook for 5 minutes until soft. Add the curry paste and cook, stirring, for 1 minute. Open the can of coconut milk and scoop off the thick cream that will have risen to the top. Add the coconut cream to the pan with the fish sauce, lime juice and sugar. Cook, stirring frequently, for 1–2 minutes. Stir in the remaining coconut milk and bring the mixture to the boil. Reduce the heat to low and simmer, stirring occasionally, for a further 5 minutes, or until the sauce thickens. Remove from the heat and leave to cool slightly. Transfer the mixture to a food processor, add the basil and coriander and process until smooth and bright green. Return the sauce to the pan and reheat over a medium–low heat.

2. Cook the noodles according to the packet instructions and place them in a large serving bowl.

3. Add the chicken and sauce to the noodles and toss to combine. Serve immediately, garnished with the spring onions.

TURKEY MEATBALLS WITH GINGER-SOBA NOODLES

SERVES: 4   **PREP TIME: 15 MINS**   **COOK TIME: 20 MINS**

INGREDIENTS

cooking spray, for greasing
450 g/1 lb fresh turkey mince
1 egg, lightly beaten
4 spring onions, finely chopped
3 garlic cloves
25 g/1 oz fresh coriander, finely chopped
70 g/2½ oz water chestnuts, finely diced
2 tbsp soy sauce
1 tbsp sesame oil
½ tsp salt
75 g/2¾ oz panko breadcrumbs
225 g/8 oz dried soba noodles

SAUCE

4 spring onions, finely chopped
55 g/2 oz fresh ginger, very finely chopped
¾ tsp salt
4 tbsp groundnut oil

1. Preheat the oven to 200°C/400°F/Gas Mark 6. Line a baking tray with baking paper and spray it with cooking spray.

2. Combine the turkey, egg, spring onions, garlic, coriander, water chestnuts, soy sauce, sesame oil, salt and breadcrumbs in a medium-sized bowl. Mix well with a fork or your hands, but do not overwork the mixture. Shape the mixture into 4-cm/1½-inch balls and place them on the prepared baking tray, spaced well apart. Continue until all of the meat mixture has been shaped into balls. Lightly spray the tops of the meatballs with cooking spray and bake in the preheated oven for 20 minutes, or until cooked through and beginning to brown.

3. Meanwhile, cook the noodles according to the packet instructions. Place in a large serving bowl.

4. To make the sauce, combine the spring onions, ginger and salt in a medium-sized heatproof bowl. Heat the oil in a small saucepan over a high heat until just beginning to smoke. Carefully pour the hot oil over the spring onion mixture and stir with a fork.

5. Add the cooked meatballs to the noodles in the bowl, then add the sauce and toss to coat well. Serve immediately.

CHICKEN WITH UDON NOODLES & PEANUTS

SERVES: 4　　　　**PREP TIME: 10 MINS**　　　　**COOK TIME: 5 MINS**

INGREDIENTS

350 g/12 oz fresh udon noodles

1 garlic clove, finely chopped

175 g/6 oz smooth peanut butter

3 tbsp reduced-salt soy sauce

3 tbsp unseasoned rice vinegar

2 tbsp soft light brown sugar

2 tsp toasted sesame oil

1 tsp chilli paste or ¼ tsp cayenne pepper

2–3 tbsp water (optional)

350 g/12 oz cooked chicken, shredded

1 cucumber, peeled, deseeded and cut into matchsticks

1 red pepper, deseeded and cut into matchsticks

3 tbsp finely chopped fresh coriander, to garnish

1. Cook the noodles according to the packet instructions.

2. Meanwhile, put the garlic into a food processor with the peanut butter, soy sauce, vinegar, sugar, oil and chilli paste and process until smooth and well combined. Add the water, a little at a time, until the desired consistency is reached.

3. Drain the noodles and place them in a large bowl. Add the sauce and toss until well coated. Add the chicken, cucumber and red pepper and toss again to combine. Serve immediately, garnished with coriander.

 HERO TIPS

For the best flavour, use all-natural peanut butter that is made from nothing but peanuts or peanuts and salt.

SESAME SOBA NOODLES WITH GRILLED CHICKEN

SERVES: 4   **PREP TIME: 25 MINS, PLUS MARINATING**   **COOK TIME: 20 MINS**

INGREDIENTS

zest and juice of 1 large orange
1 tbsp soft dark brown sugar
1 tbsp rice vinegar
1 tbsp soy sauce
1 garlic clove, finely chopped
1 tbsp finely chopped fresh ginger
450 g/1 lb boneless, skinless chicken breasts, cut into strips
350 g/12 oz dried soba noodles
115 g/4 oz sugar snap peas, halved crossways
6 small radishes, thinly sliced
4 spring onions, thinly sliced, to garnish

SESAME SAUCE

1 garlic clove, peeled
2.5-cm/1-inch piece fresh ginger, peeled
70 g/2½ oz tahini
2 tbsp soft dark brown sugar
2 tbsp soy sauce
2 tbsp sesame oil
1 tbsp rice vinegar
¼–½ tsp hot chilli oil
1–2 tbsp lukewarm water

1. Combine the orange zest and juice, sugar, vinegar, soy sauce, garlic and ginger in a medium-sized bowl. Add the chicken and toss to coat. Marinate for at least 30 minutes or overnight.

2. Cook the noodles according to the packet instructions. Drain and keep warm.

3. Preheat the grill to high. Remove the chicken strips from the marinade (discarding the marinade), and cook under the grill for about 4 minutes on each side, until cooked through.

4. To make the sesame sauce, process the garlic and ginger in a blender or food processor until finely chopped. Add the tahini, sugar, soy sauce, sesame oil, vinegar and chilli oil and process until smooth. Add the water, a little at a time, until the desired consistency is achieved.

5. Pour the sauce over the warm noodles and toss to coat. Add the sugar snap peas and radishes and toss to combine. Serve the noodles topped with the strips of chicken and garnished with the spring onions.

TURKEY WITH CORIANDER PESTO & SOBA NOODLES

SERVES: 6-8

PREP TIME: 10 MINS, PLUS MARINATING

COOK TIME: 20 MINS

INGREDIENTS

4 tbsp reduced-salt soy sauce

2 tsp chilli paste

3 garlic cloves, sliced

1 boneless, skinless turkey breast, about 1.3–1.8 kg/3–4 lb

450 g/1 lb dried soba noodles

PESTO

85 g/3 oz fresh coriander, chopped

125 ml/4 fl oz vegetable oil

50 g/1¾ oz sugar

4 garlic cloves

2 tbsp finely chopped fresh ginger

2 tsp chilli paste

juice of 1 lime

2 tsp salt

1. Combine the soy sauce, chilli paste and garlic in a bowl large enough to hold the turkey breast. Add the turkey breast and turn to coat. Cover and marinate in the refrigerator for at least 2 hours or overnight.

2. To cook the turkey, allow it to come to room temperature and preheat the grill to high. Grill for about 10 minutes on each side, until a meat thermometer inserted into the thickest part registers 75°C/165°F.

3. Meanwhile, cook the noodles according to the packet instructions. Drain and set aside.

4. To make the pesto, combine the coriander, oil, sugar, garlic, ginger, chilli paste, lime juice and salt in a food processor and process until well combined.

5. Remove the cooked turkey from the grill, loosely cover with foil and leave to rest for at least 5 minutes before slicing.

6. Toss the noodles with the pesto and slice the turkey into 5-mm/¼-inch slices. Serve immediately with the noodles.

FROM THE FARM

PORK RAMEN SOUP

SERVES: 4 **PREP TIME: 10 MINS, PLUS MARINATING** **COOK TIME: 1 HR**

INGREDIENTS

1 tbsp finely chopped fresh ginger

2 tbsp clear honey

2 tbsp soy sauce

2 tbsp mirin

1 tsp sesame oil

1 tsp Chinese five spice

1 pork fillet, about 675 g/1 lb 8 oz

beansprouts, pea shoots and hard-boiled eggs, to garnish

SOUP

1 tbsp vegetable oil

1 yellow onion, diced

3 garlic cloves, finely chopped

1 tbsp grated fresh ginger

1.5 litres/2¾ pints chicken stock

225 g/8 oz fresh shiitake mushrooms, stems removed and caps thinly sliced

½ tsp rock salt

4 tsp reduced-salt soy sauce

1 tablespoon Chinese rice wine

1 tsp sesame oil

500 g/1 lb 2 oz dried ramen noodles

4 tsp miso paste

1. To prepare the pork, stir together the ginger, honey, soy sauce, mirin, sesame oil and five spice in a large bowl. Add the pork and turn to coat. Cover and refrigerate for at least 2 hours or overnight.

2. To make the soup, heat the vegetable oil in a large saucepan over a medium–high heat. Add the onion, garlic and ginger and cook, stirring, for 5 minutes, or until the onions are soft and translucent. Add the stock, mushrooms, salt, soy sauce, wine and sesame oil and bring to the boil. Reduce the heat to low and simmer, uncovered, for about 30 minutes.

3. Meanwhile, preheat the oven to 190°C/375°F/Gas Mark 5. Place the pork on a baking tray and roast in the preheated oven for 20 minutes.

4. Meanwhile, preheat the barbecue to high. Transfer the pork to the grill rack and cook for about 5 minutes on each side, until brown and beginning to show grill marks. Reduce the heat to medium–low and continue to cook until a meat thermometer inserted into the thickest part of the meat registers a temperature of 63–68°C/145–155°F. Remove from the barbecue, loosely cover with foil, and leave to rest for 5 minutes before slicing.

5. Bring the soup back to the boil and add the noodles, breaking them up to ensure that they are all submerged in the liquid. Cook for about 3 minutes, until the noodles are tender. Stir in the miso paste until fully dissolved.

6. Thinly slice the pork. Ladle the soup into bowls, top with several slices of pork, garnish with the beansprouts, pea shoots and hard-boiled eggs and serve immediately.

RAMEN MEATBALL SOUP

SERVES: 4   **PREP TIME: 15 MINS**   **COOK TIME: 50 MINS**

INGREDIENTS
MEATBALLS

cooking spray, for greasing
450 g/1 lb fresh beef mince
75 g/2¾ oz panko
breadcrumbs
1 egg, lightly beaten
1 tbsp finely chopped
fresh ginger
2 garlic cloves, finely chopped
3 spring onions,
finely chopped
1 tsp salt
1 tsp sesame oil

SOUP

1 tbsp vegetable oil
2 garlic cloves, finely chopped
1 tbsp grated fresh ginger
1.5 litres/2¾ pints beef stock
4 tbsp soy sauce
1 tbsp sake or dry white wine
1 tsp salt
1 tsp sesame oil
500 g/1 lb 2 oz dried ramen
noodles (flavouring sachet
discarded, if included)
4 spring onions, thinly sliced,
to garnish

1. Preheat the oven to 200°C/400°F/Gas Mark 6. Line a large baking tray with baking paper and lightly spritz it with cooking spray.

2. To make the meatballs, combine the beef, panko, egg, ginger, garlic, spring onions, salt and oil in a large bowl and mix well. Shape the mixture into 2.5-cm/1-inch balls, placing them on the prepared baking tray as you go. Bake in the preheated oven for 12–14 minutes until lightly browned and cooked through.

3. To make the soup, heat the vegetable oil in a large saucepan over a medium–high heat. Add the garlic and ginger and cook, stirring, for about 3 minutes until soft. Add the stock, soy sauce, sake, salt and sesame oil and bring to the boil. Reduce the heat to low and simmer, uncovered, for about 30 minutes. Add the meatballs.

4. Bring the soup back to the boil and add the noodles, breaking them up to ensure that they are all submerged in the liquid. Cook for about 3 minutes, until the noodles are soft. Serve hot, garnished with spring onions.

STEAK & SOBA NOODLE SALAD

SERVES: 4

PREP TIME: 15 MINS, PLUS MARINATING

COOK TIME: 10 MINS

INGREDIENTS

2 tbsp soy sauce

1 tbsp Chinese rice wine, dry sherry or dry white wine

2 garlic cloves, finely chopped

2 tsp soft light brown sugar

2 tbsp olive oil

1 sirloin steak, about 450 g/1 lb

40 g/1½ oz toasted sesame seeds, to garnish

DRESSING

juice of 1 lime

2 tbsp white miso paste

1 tbsp reduced-salt soy sauce

1 tbsp unseasoned rice vinegar

4 tbsp vegetable oil

1 tbsp sesame oil

SALAD

350 g/12 oz dried soba noodles

½ large cucumber

100 g/3½ oz rocket

10 g/¼ oz chopped fresh coriander

3 spring onions, thinly sliced

1. Combine the soy sauce, wine, garlic, sugar and olive oil in a large bowl. Add the steak and turn to coat. Refrigerate for at least 2 hours or overnight.

2. To cook the steak, preheat the grill to high. Remove the steak from the marinade (discarding the marinade), place under the grill and cook for 4–5 minutes on each side for medium-rare, or a few minutes longer if you prefer your steak more well done. Remove from the grill, loosely cover with foil and leave to rest for at least 5 minutes. Slice the steak into 5-mm/¼ -inch thick slices.

3. Meanwhile, prepare the dressing. Combine the lime juice, miso paste, soy sauce and rice vinegar in a small bowl and whisk to combine. Add the vegetable oil and sesame oil and whisk until the dressing is emulsified.

4. To make the salad, cook the noodles according to the packet instructions, drain and cool. Peel the cucumber and cut in half lengthways, deseed and finely slice. Place in a bowl with the remaining salad ingredients, add some dressing and toss to combine and coat.

5. To serve, divide the salad between individual serving plates and top each with several slices of steak. Drizzle a little dressing over the steak and garnish with the sesame seeds.

SICHUAN NUMBING BEEF SALAD

SERVES: 4
PREP TIME: 10 MINS, PLUS MARINATING
COOK TIME: 10 MINS

INGREDIENTS

350 g/12 oz sirloin steak
90 g/3¼ oz egg noodles
1 small red onion, halved and thinly sliced into crescents
6 radishes, sliced
4 good handfuls of peppery leaves such as tatsoi, mustard greens and rocket
1½ tbsp groundnut oil
1 tsp Sichuan pepper, crushed

MARINADE

4 tsp Chinese rice wine or dry sherry
½ tbsp soy sauce
4 tsp sugar
2 tbsp hoisin sauce
2.5-cm/1-inch piece fresh ginger, squeezed in a garlic press

DRESSING

2 tsp Sichuan pepper, crushed
1½ tbsp light soy sauce
1½ tbsp rice vinegar
2 tbsp cold-pressed sesame oil

1. Trim any fat from the steaks. Slice the meat into thin strips and put in a shallow dish. Combine the marinade ingredients and pour over the beef. Leave to marinate for 30 minutes.

2. Cook the noodles according to the packet instructions. Drain, allow to cool and snip into shorter lengths. Whisk the dressing ingredients until well blended. Combine the noodles, onion, radishes and salad leaves in a large bowl. Whisk the dressing again and pour two thirds of it over the salad. Toss to distribute the noodles, then divide between individual serving plates.

3. Heat a wok over a medium–high heat, then add the groundnut oil and the Sichuan pepper. Stir for a few seconds to flavour the oil. Add the beef and marinade, and stir-fry for 4–5 minutes until caramelized. Remove with a slotted spoon, and scatter over the salad. Pour over the remaining dressing. Serve immediately.

1

2

3

KNOW YOUR NOODLES!
(DIFFERENT TYPES OF NOODLES)

Generally noodles are sold in three basic formats; ready cooked (sold both in the chiller cabinet and as an ambient product), dried and fresh.

Of course the choice you make depends on where you might be shopping and how much time you have available. The dried and long life pre-cooked noodles are the most convenient.

With regards to the different types of noodles available, there are many varieties, but we will concentrate on the following:

Soba
Ramen
Udon
Rice
Egg

SOBA

Generally soba are made with buckwheat flour (although they can also be bought made with rice flour). Unlike its name suggests buckwheat contains no gluten or wheat. Soba noodles can contain between 40-100% buckwheat, the rest of the flour used being wheat. It's the buckwheat that gives the noodles their distinctive colour and nuttiness. Soba are the most popular noodles in Japan and come in a variety of thicknesses.

RAMEN

In Japan, ramen is seen as comfort food and is hugely popular. Whether its origins are from China or Japan are unknown, but there are many regional specialities, and restaurants devoted to ramen-based meals cooked by chefs who specialize in the cooking techniques associated with ramen.

Ramen generally relates to a broth-based dish in which Chukamen noodles are served, made with wheat flour. There are other uses for ramen noodles, for example the ramen burger. This uses cooked noodles, pressed into patty shapes and then fried in place of a bread roll for a completely new burger eating experience!

UDON

Generally thick and white, these noodles are made with a semi whole-wheat flour. They are light and easily digested and the slow drying time helps give them a good flavour. They are sold in different thicknesses; and work best in soups and broths but can also be used just as any other noodle.

RICE

Made from rice flour and water these wiry thin noodles are common in South East Asia and Southern China. They are sold in a variety of thicknesses and are also available made with brown rice flour. The same dough is used to make rice wrappers. They are perfect for use in stir-fries, soups and salads.

EGG

Made with wheat flour, water and eggs (can be duck eggs). They vary in width and colour, from a pale cream to deep yellow depending on the amount of egg content. Generally they cook fast and are a good all-purpose noodle.

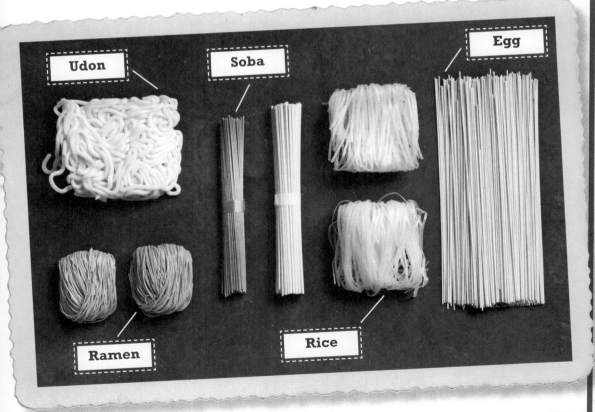

Udon

Soba

Egg

Ramen

Rice

RAMEN BURGER

SERVES: 2

PREP TIME: 10 MINS, PLUS CHILLING

COOK TIME: 15 MINS

INGREDIENTS
NOODLE BUN

175 g/6 oz ramen noodles (flavouring sachet discarded, if included), cooked according to the packet instructions, rinsed, drained and left to dry

2 eggs, lightly beaten

2 spring onions, thinly sliced

2 tbsp vegetable oil

BURGER

225 g/8 oz fresh beef mince

1 tsp grated fresh ginger

2 spring onions, thinly sliced

1 tbsp hoisin sauce

2 tsp sriracha sauce

1 tsp reduced-salt soy sauce

1½ tsp sesame oil

TO SERVE

50 g/1¾ oz cabbage, shredded

2 tbsp finely chopped fresh coriander

hoisin sauce, sriracha or ketchup (optional)

1. Combine the noodles, eggs and spring onions in a bowl and stir to mix. Place an equal amount of the noodle mixture in each of four flat bowls with a diameter of 10–13 cm/4–5 inches. Place clingfilm over the surface of the bowls and place a heavy glass or can in the bowls to weigh the noodles down. Chill in the refrigerator for about 30 minutes.

2. Meanwhile, to make the burger, combine the beef with the ginger, spring onions, hoisin sauce, sriracha sauce, soy sauce and sesame oil in a bowl and mix well. Shape the mixture into 2 patties.

3. To cook the burgers, preheat the grill to medium. Place the patties under the grill and cook for 4–5 minutes on each side, or until cooked to your liking.

4. To cook the buns, heat the oil in a large non-stick frying pan over a medium–high heat. Remove the chilled noodle buns from the bowls and place in the pan and cook on each side for 5 minutes, or until brown and crisp.

5. To serve, place each burger on one of the noodle buns. Top with cabbage, coriander, and hoisin sauce, if using. Add the bun lid and serve.

PORK & NOODLES IN PLUM SAUCE

With its tangy sweet-sour flavour, plum sauce is a great combination with pork.

MAKES: 4   **PREP TIME: 10 MINS**   **COOK TIME: 10-12 MINS**

INGREDIENTS

600 g/1 lb 5 oz pork fillet
2 tbsp groundnut oil
1 orange pepper, deseeded and sliced
1 bunch spring onions, sliced
250 g/9 oz oyster mushrooms, sliced
300 g/10½ oz fresh beansprouts
2 tbsp dry sherry
150 ml/5 fl oz plum sauce
250 g/9 oz medium egg noodles
salt and pepper
chopped fresh coriander, to garnish

1. Slice the pork into long, thin strips. Heat a wok over a medium–high heat, then add the oil. Add the pork strips and stir-fry for 2–3 minutes until cooked through.

2. Add the orange pepper and stir-fry for 2 minutes, then add the spring onions, mushrooms and beansprouts.

3. Stir-fry for 2–3 minutes, then add the sherry and plum sauce and heat until boiling. Season well with salt and pepper.

4. Meanwhile, cook the noodles according to the packet instructions. Drain, then add to the wok and toss well. Serve immediately, garnished with the fresh coriander.

HERO TIPS

For a spicier version of this dish, simply add 2 tablespoons of chilli sauce along with the sherry and plum sauce.

MINTY LAMB MEATBALLS WITH SOBA NOODLES

SERVES: 4   **PREP TIME: 25 MINS**   **COOK TIME: 15 MINS**

INGREDIENTS
MEATBALLS

cooking spray, for greasing

450 g/1 lb fresh lamb mince

1 shallot, finely chopped

2 garlic cloves, finely chopped

1 tbsp each, finely chopped
fresh mint leaves and
coriander leaves

2 serrano chillies, deseeded
and chopped

1 tbsp Thai fish sauce

75 g/2¾ oz panko breadcrumbs

1 egg

350 g/12 oz dried soba noodles

35 g/1¼ oz crushed
dry-roasted peanuts,
to garnish

PESTO

2 serrano chillies

2.5-cm/1–inch piece fresh
ginger

4 garlic cloves

55 g/2 oz fresh mint leaves

10 g/¼ oz fresh basil leaves

juice of 1 lime

1 tbsp Thai fish sauce

1 tbsp sugar

3 tbsp vegetable oil

1. Preheat the oven to 200°C/400°F/Gas Mark 6. Line a large baking tray with baking paper and spray it with cooking spray.

2. To make the meatballs, combine the lamb, shallot, garlic, mint, coriander, chillies, fish sauce, panko and egg and mix well. Shape the meat mixture into 4-cm/1½-inch balls and place them on the prepared tray. Lightly spritz the tops with cooking spray and bake in the preheated oven for 15 minutes, or until cooked through.

3. Meanwhile, to make the pesto, halve and deseed the chillies and peel and chop the ginger. Place into a food processor with the garlic and process until finely chopped. Add the mint, basil, lime juice, fish sauce, sugar and oil and process to a smooth purée.

4. Cook the noodles according to the packet instructions. Drain and toss the noodles with the pesto in a large bowl. Serve immediately topped with meatballs and garnished with peanuts.

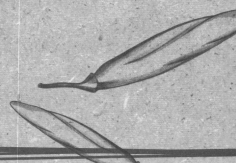

SESAME UDON NOODLES WITH STIR-FRIED BEEF

SERVES: 4   **PREP TIME: 15 MINS, PLUS MARINATING**   **COOK TIME: 10 MINS**

INGREDIENTS

1 tbsp sugar
1 tbsp soy sauce
1 tbsp sesame oil
450 g/1 lb sirloin steak, thinly sliced
450 g/1 lb fresh udon noodles
2 tbsp vegetable oil
2 tbsp toasted sesame seeds and 3 thinly sliced spring onions, to garnish

SESAME SAUCE

1 garlic clove, peeled
2-5-cm/1-inch piece fresh ginger, peeled
4 tbsp tahini
2 tbsp soft dark brown sugar
2 tbsp soy sauce
2 tbsp sesame oil
1 tbsp rice vinegar
¼ –½ tsp hot chilli oil
1–2 tbsp lukewarm water

1. Combine the sugar, soy sauce and sesame oil in a medium-sized bowl. Add the beef, stir to coat, and leave to marinate for about 30 minutes.

2. Meanwhile, to make the sesame sauce, place the garlic and ginger in a blender or food processor and process until finely chopped. Add the tahini, sugar, soy sauce, sesame oil, vinegar and chilli oil and process until smooth. Add the water, a little at a time, until the desired consistency is achieved.

3. Cook the noodles according to the packet instructions, drain, and keep warm.

4. Heat the vegetable oil in a large frying pan over a medium–high heat. Remove the beef from the marinade (discarding the marinade) and add it to the hot pan. Stir-fry, stirring frequently, for about 4 minutes, until brown and cooked through.

5. In a large bowl, toss the noodles with some of the sauce until well coated. Divide the noodles between four serving plates and top with some of the beef. Drizzle a little more sesame sauce over the beef and serve, garnished with sesame seeds and spring onions.

DAN DAN NOODLES WITH PORK MINCE

SERVES: 4 **PREP TIME: 5 MINS** **COOK TIME: 15 MINS**

INGREDIENTS

450 g/1 lb fresh udon noodles
1 tbsp vegetable oil
350 g/12 oz fresh pork mince
½ tsp salt
¼ tsp pepper
2 tbsp finely chopped fresh ginger
175 ml/6 fl oz chicken stock
4 tbsp tahini
2 tbsp rice vinegar
2 tbsp soy sauce
2 tbsp soft light brown sugar
2–3 tsp chilli oil
1 tsp sesame oil
1 tsp crushed Sichuan peppercorns
2 tbsp chopped roasted peanuts and 3 spring onions, thinly sliced, to garnish

1. Cook the noodles according to the packet instructions. Drain and set aside.

2. Heat the oil in a large frying pan over a medium–high heat. Add the pork, salt and pepper and cook, stirring and breaking the meat up with a spatula, until brown all over.

3. Add the ginger and cook, stirring, for a further 1–2 minutes until fragrant. Add the stock, tahini, vinegar, soy sauce, sugar, chilli oil, sesame oil and peppercorns and bring to the boil, stirring to mix well. Simmer for 5 minutes, or until the sauce thickens.

4. Toss the noodles and sauce together in a large bowl. Serve immediately, garnished with peanuts and spring onions.

HERO TIPS

If you cannot find tahini, or simply don't like it, you can substitute with smooth peanut butter instead.

HO FUN NOODLES WITH BEEF STRIPS

Ho fun, meaning 'rice noodles', are popular in Vietnam and Thailand.

SERVES: 4

PREP TIME: 10 MINS, PLUS STANDING

COOK TIME: 5-10 MINS

INGREDIENTS

300 g/10½ oz rump or sirloin beef

2 tbsp soy sauce

2 tbsp toasted sesame oil

250 g/9 oz flat rice noodles

2 tbsp groundnut oil

1 onion, sliced into thin wedges

2 garlic cloves, crushed

2.5-cm/1-inch piece fresh ginger, chopped

1 red chilli, thinly sliced

200 g/7 oz sprouting broccoli

½ Chinese leaves, sliced

chilli oil, to serve

1. Slice the beef into thin strips, place in a bowl and sprinkle with the soy sauce and toasted sesame oil. Cover and leave to stand for 15 minutes.

2. Prepare the noodles according to the packet instructions. Drain and set aside.

3. Heat a wok over a high heat, then add 1 tablespoon of groundnut oil. Add the beef and stir-fry until evenly coloured. Remove and keep to one side.

4. Add the remaining oil and stir-fry the onion, garlic, ginger and chilli for 1 minute.

5. Add the broccoli and stir-fry for 2 minutes, then add the leaves and stir-fry for 1 minute. Serve the noodles, beef and vegetables immediately, drizzled with chilli oil.

PORK PAD THAI

SERVES: 4　　　　**PREP TIME: 10 MINS**　　　　**COOK TIME: 6-10 MINS**

INGREDIENTS

225 g/8 oz thick dried
rice noodles

2 tbsp groundnut or
vegetable oil

4 spring onions,
roughly chopped

2 garlic cloves, crushed

2 red chillies, deseeded
and sliced

225 g/8 oz pork fillet, trimmed
and thinly sliced

115 g/4 oz cooked peeled
large prawns

juice of 1 lime

2 tbsp Thai fish sauce

2 eggs, beaten

55 g/2 oz fresh beansprouts

handful of chopped
fresh coriander

55 g/2 oz unsalted
peanuts, chopped

lime wedges, to serve

1. Prepare the noodles according to the packet instructions. Drain and set aside.

2. Heat a wok over a medium–high heat, then add the oil. Add the spring onions, garlic and chillies and stir-fry for 1–2 minutes. Add the pork and stir-fry over a high heat for 1–2 minutes until cooked through.

3. Add the prawns, lime juice, fish sauce and eggs and stir-fry over a medium heat for 2–3 minutes until the eggs have set and the prawns are heated through.

4. Add the beansprouts, most of the coriander, the peanuts and the noodles and stir-fry for 30 seconds until heated through. Garnish with the remaining coriander and serve immediately with lime wedges.

HERO TIPS

This traditional Thai dish has many variations but should always include noodles and peanuts. It is important to use thick rice noodles, which are now widely available.

LAMB & PUMPKIN CURRY WITH UDON NOODLES

Udon noodles are perfect for soaking up this rich, spicy sauce. Full-flavoured lamb makes this dish especially satisfying, but you can also substitute beef, pork or chicken.

SERVES: 4   **PREP TIME: 10 MINS**   **COOK TIME: 30 MINS**

INGREDIENTS

2 tbsp vegetable oil

2 shallots, thinly sliced

450 g/1 lb lamb shoulder, cut into 2.5-cm/1-inch cubes

1–2 tbsp red Thai curry paste

400 ml/14 fl oz canned coconut milk

225 ml/8 fl oz vegetable, beef or chicken stock or water

3 tbsp Thai fish sauce

2 tbsp soft light brown sugar

3 lemon grass stalks, cut into 7.5-cm/3-inch pieces and bruised with the side of a heavy knife

3 kaffir lime leaves, julienned

260 g/9 oz pumpkin, or butternut squash, peeled and cut into 2.5-cm/ 1-inch cubes

350 g/12 oz dried udon noodles

juice of 1 lime

10 g/¼ oz chopped fresh coriander, to garnish

1. Heat the oil in a large, deep frying pan over a medium–high heat. Add the shallots and cook, stirring frequently, for 5 minutes, or until soft. Add the lamb and cook, stirring frequently, until brown all over. Stir in the curry paste and about 2 tablespoons of the thick cream at the top of the can of coconut milk. Cook for 1 minute. Add the remaining coconut milk, the stock, fish sauce, sugar, lemon grass and lime leaves. Bring to the boil and add the pumpkin. Reduce the heat to medium–low, cover and simmer for 15–20 minutes, until the pumpkin is tender.

2. Meanwhile, cook the noodles according to the packet instructions. Drain and set aside.

3. When the pumpkin is tender, add the drained noodles to the frying pan and cook for 2–3 minutes, until heated through. Stir in the lime juice and serve immediately, garnished with coriander.

FROM THE SEA

SALMON RAMEN

SERVES: 4   **PREP TIME: 10-15 MINS**   **COOK TIME: 10-15 MINS**

INGREDIENTS

1 litre/1¾ pints fish or
vegetable stock

1 large garlic clove

½ tsp light soy sauce

4 salmon fillets, about
140 g/5 oz each, skinned

groundnut or sunflower oil,
for brushing

140 g/5 oz dried ramen or fine
egg noodles

100 g/3½ oz baby
spinach leaves

4 spring onions, chopped

TERIYAKI GLAZE

2½ tbsp sake

2½ tbsp dark soy sauce

2 tbsp mirin or sweet sherry

½ tbsp soft light brown sugar

½ garlic clove, very
finely chopped

5-mm/¼-inch piece fresh
ginger, very finely chopped

TO SERVE

100 g/3½ oz fresh beansprouts

1 fresh green chilli, deseeded
and sliced

fresh coriander leaves

1. Preheat the grill to high. Put the stock in a saucepan, add the garlic clove and soy sauce and bring to the boil.

2. Mix together the ingredients for the teriyaki glaze and brush one surface of each salmon fillet with the glaze. Lightly brush the grill rack with oil and cook the salmon under the preheated grill for 4 minutes on one side only. The flesh should flake easily and the centre should remain a bright pink. Remove the fish from the grill and set aside.

3. Cook the noodles according to the packet instructions. Drain and set aside.

4. Remove the garlic from the stock, then bring the stock back to the boil. Drop in the spinach leaves and spring onions and cook until the leaves are just wilted. Use a slotted spoon to remove the spinach and spring onions from the pan and divide them among warmed bowls. Divide the noodles among the bowls, then add a salmon fillet to each. Carefully pour the boiling stock into each bowl.

5. Sprinkle with the beansprouts, chilli slices and coriander leaves and serve immediately.

SPICY UDON NOODLES & PRAWNS

SERVES: 4

PREP TIME: 15 MINS, PLUS MARINATING

COOK TIME: 35 MINS

INGREDIENTS

2 tbsp vegetable oil

2 leeks, halved lengthways and thinly sliced

2 garlic cloves, finely chopped

2 lemon grass stalks, pounded with the side of a heavy knife and cut into 5-cm/ 2-inch lengths

2 hot red chillies, sliced into rings

1 tsp salt

1.5 litres/2¾ pints vegetable stock

grated zest and juice of 1 lime

6 kaffir lime leaves

350 g/12 oz fresh udon noodles

shredded red cabbage and shredded carrot, to garnish

PRAWNS

1 tbsp finely chopped fresh ginger

2 garlic cloves, finely chopped

125 ml/4 fl oz soy sauce

4 tbsp lime juice

1 tbsp sugar

2 tbsp vegetable oil

450 g/1 lb raw prawns, peeled and deveined

1. Heat the oil in a large saucepan over a medium–high heat. Add the leeks and cook, stirring, for about 5 minutes, until soft. Add the garlic, lemon grass, chillies and salt and cook for a further minute. Add the stock, lime zest and juice and lime leaves and bring to the boil. Reduce the heat and simmer for about 20 minutes. Remove the lemon grass pieces and lime leaves.

2. Meanwhile, soak 8 wooden skewers in water until needed. Whisk together the ginger, garlic, soy sauce, lime juice and sugar in a medium-sized bowl. Add the vegetable oil and whisk to emulsify. Add the prawns and toss to coat. Leave to marinate at room temperature for about 15 minutes.

3. Preheat the grill to high. Remove the prawns from the marinade and thread them onto the pre-soaked skewers. Place under the grill and cook for about 2 minutes on each side, until the prawns are pink and cooked through.

4. Bring the soup back to a low boil, add the noodles, reduce the heat and simmer for about 5 minutes until the noodles are tender.

5. Divide the soup between warmed bowls, top each portion with shredded carrot and cabbage and 2 prawn skewers and serve immediately.

SOBA NOODLE NICOISE SALAD

SERVES: 4　　　　**PREP TIME: 25 MINS**　　　　**COOK TIME: 2 MINS**

INGREDIENTS

1 tbsp vegetable oil
450 g/1 lb sushi grade ahi tuna
35 g/1¼ oz black sesame seeds
salt and pepper

DRESSING

4 tbsp rice wine vinegar
1 tbsp soy sauce
2 tsp wasabi paste
125 ml/4 fl oz vegetable oil

SALAD

350 g/12 oz dried soba noodles, cooked according to the packet instructions
225 g/8 oz French beans, blanched in lightly salted boiling water until soft but still firm to the bite
4 hard-boiled eggs, sliced
12 cherry tomatoes, halved
55 g/2 oz thinly sliced pickled ginger

1. Heat the oil in a large frying pan over a high heat. Season the tuna steaks on both sides with salt and pepper. Spread the sesame seeds on a plate in a thin layer. Press the pieces of tuna onto the sesame seeds to coat both sides. When the oil begins to shimmer, add the pieces of tuna. Cook for about 1 minute on each side, until the outside of the fish begins to brown and there is just a thin layer of opaqueness at the edge. The centre of the tuna should still be pink. Remove from the pan and leave to rest for several minutes, then cut into 5-mm/¼-inch thick slices and chill in the refrigerator while you prepare the rest of the dish.

2. To make the dressing, combine the vinegar, soy sauce and wasabi paste in a small bowl and whisk to combine. Add the oil and whisk until emulsified.

3. To make the salad, place the noodles in a large bowl and toss with some of the dressing until well coated. In a separate bowl, toss the beans with some of the dressing. Divide the noodles, beans, eggs, tomatoes, ginger and sliced tuna between serving plates. Drizzle a little dressing over the tuna slices and serve immediately.

UDON NOODLE STIR-FRY WITH FISH CAKE & GINGER

Made with puréed white fish, Japanese fish cake comes pre-rolled ready for slicing.

SERVES: 2   **PREP TIME: 10 MINS**   **COOK TIME: 5–10 MINS**

INGREDIENTS

2 x 150-g/5½-oz packs ready-to-wok udon noodles

1 leek, shredded

200 g/7 oz beansprouts

8 shiitake mushrooms, finely sliced

2 pieces Japanese fish cake, sliced

12 raw prawns, peeled and deveined

2 eggs, beaten

1 tbsp groundnut or vegetable oil

2 tbsp shoyu (Japanese soy sauce)

3 tbsp mirin

2 tbsp chopped fresh coriander leaves

TO SERVE

chilli oil

2 spring onions, finely sliced

2 tbsp shredded beni-shoga (red ginger)

1. Rinse the noodles under cold running water to remove any oil and tip into a bowl.

2. Add the leek, beansprouts, mushrooms, fish cake, prawns and eggs to the noodles and mix well to combine.

3. Heat a wok over a high heat. Add a little oil and heat until very hot. Add the noodle mixture and stir-fry until golden and the prawns turn pink and start to curl. Add the shoyu, mirin and coriander and toss together.

4. Divide the noodles between two bowls and drizzle with the chilli oil. Sprinkle with the spring onions and beni-shoga and serve immediately.

STIR-FRIED RICE NOODLES WITH MARINATED FISH

A tangy chilli, lime and fish sauce marinade adds sensational flavour to this impressive dish.

MAKES: 4

PREP TIME: 10 MINS, PLUS MARINATING

COOK TIME: 5 MINS

INGREDIENTS

450 g/1 lb monkfish or cod, cubed

225 g/8 oz salmon fillets, cubed

115 g/4 oz thick rice noodles

2 tbsp vegetable or groundnut oil

2 shallots, sliced

2 garlic cloves, finely chopped

1 fresh red chilli, deseeded and chopped

2 tbsp Thai soy sauce

2 tbsp chilli sauce

sprigs of fresh coriander, to garnish

MARINADE

2 tbsp vegetable or groundnut oil

2 fresh green chillies, deseeded and chopped

grated rind and juice of 1 lime

1 tbsp fish sauce

1. Combine the marinade ingredients and pour over the fish. Leave to marinate for 2 hours.

2. Prepare the noodles according to the packet instructions. Drain and set aside.

3. Heat a wok over a medium–high heat and add the oil. Sauté the shallots, garlic and red chilli until lightly browned. Add the soy sauce and chilli sauce. Add the fish and the marinade to the wok and stir-fry gently for 2–3 minutes until cooked through.

4. Add the noodles and stir gently. Garnish with coriander and serve immediately.

MISO-GLAZED COD WITH SOBA NOODLES

This sweet and salty miso glaze is simple to make, but adds a rich flavour that nicely complements a mild, meaty fish like cod.

SERVES: 4

PREP TIME: 5 MINS, PLUS MARINATING

COOK TIME: 12 MINS

INGREDIENTS

90 g/3¼ oz white miso paste

3 tbsp soft light brown sugar

2 tbsp mirin or sake

1–2 tbsp water, if needed

4 cod fillets, about 125 g/4½ oz each

350 g/12 oz dried soba noodles

1 tbsp sesame oil

1 tbsp toasted sesame seeds and 3 spring onions, thinly sliced, to garnish

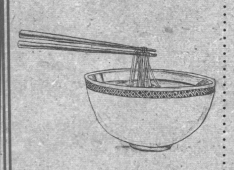

1. Combine the miso paste, sugar and mirin in a small saucepan and cook over a medium–high heat, stirring constantly, for 2 minutes, or until the mixture is just beginning to bubble. If the mixture is too thick, add 1–2 tablespoons of water.

2. Pat the fish fillets dry and place them in a single layer in a baking dish. Brush a little of the miso mixture on each fish fillet and marinate in the refrigerator for 30 minutes.

3. Cook the noodles according to the packet instructions. Drain and toss with the sesame oil.

4. Preheat the oven to 190°C/375°F/Gas Mark 5 and preheat the grill to high. Cook the fish under the grill for 4 minutes, or until the glaze begins to caramelize. Brush the remaining miso mixture on the fish and bake in the preheated oven for about 5 minutes, until the fish is cooked through and flakes easily with a fork.

5. To serve, divide the noodles between four serving plates. Top each serving with a fish fillet and garnish with sesame seeds and spring onions.

UDON IT?
(THE CLASSIC & BEST NOODLE PARTNERS)

Fresh Chillies

The smaller the chilli the hotter it is. Green varieties have more heat than the red as they sweeten as they ripen. To prepare: rinse halve and remove the seeds (unless the recipe says otherwise). Always wash the utensils before preparing other foods and do not touch your eyes whilst preparing them.

Dried Red Chillies

These are extremely hot so use with caution, or simply add to flavour cooking oil.

Ginger

Essential in so many classic dishes, this pungent, vibrant fresh tasting root adds a distinctive flavour.

Fresh root ginger is the preferred choice and always choose a root which is plump with smooth skin.

To use, simply peel away the skin and grate or finely chop. Store the prepared ginger in the refrigerator for up to 3 days or freeze in ice cube trays.

Mirin

A variety of rice wine, and similar to sake but with a lower alcohol content, this sweet Japanese condiment is often used to balance salty sauces, or in dipping sauces.

Miso

Traditional miso paste is a staple Japanese food and seasoning made by fermenting rice barley and or soya beans. This versatile ingredient adds an earthy salty flavour giving a good savoury base. It can be used as a soup or the basis for sauces or spread onto meat or fish.

White miso is fermented for less time and is sweeter and lighter making it more suitable for salad dressings, marinades or broths.

Rice Wine

Commonly used as and when you might use wine in cooking, for example in marinades and sauces, it's made by fermenting glutinous rice, yeast and spring water.

Rice Vinegar

Vinegars made from rice are widely used in Chinese cooking, there are several varieties including white rice vinegar which tends to be mild and light, the black vinegar which is still fairly mild to the red version which is sweet and spicy.

Soy Sauce

Made from soya beans, flour and water which has been fermented and aged, the sauce is the result of the distilling.

Light Soy

Although light in colour, it has more flavour and a higher salt content making it better for cooking.

Dark Soy

The longer ageing process gives this sauce its rich dark colour. It's best used as a condiment for finished dishes or as a dipping sauce.

Thai Fish Sauce

A widely used ingredient in south east Asian cuisine made by fermenting anchovies in brine. Fish sauce adds a salty note to savoury dishes. It is known as nam pla in Thailand and nuoc nam in Vietnam where it is also widely used.

CHILLI PRAWNS WITH GARLIC NOODLES

SERVES: 4 **PREP TIME: 10 MINS** **COOK TIME: 15 MINS**

INGREDIENTS

200 g/7 oz cooked king or tiger prawns, peeled

4 tbsp sweet chilli dipping sauce

4 tbsp groundnut or vegetable oil

4 spring onions, chopped

55 g/2 oz mangetout, trimmed and halved diagonally

1 tbsp Thai red curry paste

400 ml/14 fl oz coconut milk

55 g/2 oz canned bamboo shoots, drained and rinsed

55 g/2 oz fresh beansprouts

115 g/4 oz dried medium egg noodles

2 garlic cloves, crushed

handful of fresh coriander, chopped

1. Toss the prawns with the chilli sauce in a bowl. Cover and set aside.

2. Heat half the oil in a preheated wok, add the spring onions and mangetout and stir-fry over a medium–high heat for 2–3 minutes. Add the curry paste and stir well. Pour in the coconut milk and bring gently to the boil, stirring occasionally. Add the bamboo shoots and beansprouts and cook, stirring, for 1 minute. Stir in the prawns and chilli sauce, reduce the heat and simmer for 1–2 minutes until just heated through.

3. Meanwhile, cook the noodles according to the packet instructions. Drain and return to the pan.

4. Heat the remaining oil in a small non-stick frying pan, add the garlic and stir-fry over a high heat for 30 seconds. Add to the drained noodles with half the coriander and toss together until well mixed. Transfer the garlic noodles to warmed serving bowls, top with the chilli prawn mixture and serve immediately, garnished with the remaining coriander.

CHILLI ORANGE NOODLES WITH SEARED SCALLOPS

SERVES: 4 **PREP TIME: 10 MINS** **COOK TIME: 10 MINS**

INGREDIENTS

350 g/12 oz fresh udon noodles

12–16 scallops, corals removed

1 tbsp unsalted butter

1 tbsp olive oil

salt and pepper

3 spring onions, thinly sliced, to garnish

DRESSING

3 garlic cloves, finely chopped

1 tbsp finely chopped fresh ginger

zest and juice of 1 orange

4 tbsp soy sauce

90 ml/3 fl oz sweet chilli sauce

125 ml/4 fl oz vegetable oil

1. Cook the noodles according to the packet instructions. Drain and set aside.

2. To make the dressing, combine the garlic, ginger, orange zest and juice, soy sauce and sweet chilli sauce in a bowl and whisk to combine. Add the oil and whisk until emulsified.

3. Rinse the scallops, pat them dry, and season with salt and pepper. Heat the butter and oil in a large frying pan over a high heat until the butter is melted. Add the scallops and sear for about 1½ minutes on each side, until they have a golden brown crust, but are still translucent in the centre.

4. In a large bowl, toss the noodles with most of the dressing. Divide the noodles between four plates. Top each with 3–4 scallops. Drizzle a little more dressing over the scallops and serve immediately, garnished with spring onions.

HERO TIPS

To cook perfect scallops, make sure your pan is very hot and your scallops are very dry before cooking.

SINGAPORE NOODLES

SERVES: 4 **PREP TIME: 15 MINS** **COOK TIME: 15 MINS**

INGREDIENTS

200 g/7 oz fine rice noodles

1 tbsp mild, medium or hot curry paste, to taste

1 tsp ground turmeric

6 tbsp water

2 tbsp groundnut or corn oil

½ onion, very thinly sliced

2 large garlic cloves, thinly sliced

85 g/3 oz broccoli, cut into very small florets

85 g/3 oz green beans, cut into 2.5-cm/1-inch lengths

85 g/3 oz pork fillet, cut into thin strips

85 g/3 oz small cooked peeled prawns, thawed if frozen

55 g/2 oz Chinese leaves or romaine lettuce, thinly shredded

1 fresh bird's eye chilli, deseeded and thinly sliced

2 spring onions, white parts only, thinly shredded

fresh coriander, to garnish

1. Prepare the noodles according to the packet instructions. Drain and set aside. Meanwhile, put the curry paste and turmeric in a small bowl and stir in 4 tablespoons of the water, then set aside.

2. Heat a wok over a high heat, then add the oil. Add the onion and garlic and stir-fry for 1 minute, or until the onion softens. Add the broccoli and beans to the wok with the remaining water and continue stir-frying for 2 minutes. Add the pork and stir-fry for a further minute. Add the prawns, Chinese leaves and chilli to the wok and continue stir-frying for a further 2 minutes, until the pork is cooked through and the vegetables are tender, but still with a little bite. Remove from the wok and keep warm.

3. Add the spring onions, noodles and curry paste mixture to the wok. Use 2 forks to mix together the noodles and onions, and continue stir-frying for about 2 minutes, until the noodles are hot and have picked up a dark golden colour from the turmeric. Return the other ingredients to the wok and continue stir-frying for 1 minute. Serve immediately, garnished with fresh coriander.

SPICY SAUTÉED PRAWNS IN A RAMEN NOODLE NEST

A crispy noodle nest makes the perfect backdrop for succulent prawns bathed in a sweet, spicy sauce.

SERVES: 4

PREP TIME: 10 MINS, PLUS CHILLING

COOK TIME: 10 MINS

INGREDIENTS

2 tbsp Chinese rice wine or dry sherry

1 tbsp cornflour

¼ tsp salt

675 g/1 lb 8 oz peeled and deveined raw prawns

350 g/12 oz dried ramen noodles (flavouring sachet discarded, if included)

2 tbsp vegetable oil, plus extra for deep-frying

3 tbsp chicken stock

2 tbsp tomato ketchup

1 tbsp oyster sauce

1 tbsp soy sauce

1 tbsp chilli paste

2 garlic cloves, finely chopped

1 tbsp finely chopped fresh ginger

4 spring onions, thinly sliced

1. Whisk together the wine, cornflour and salt in a medium-sized bowl. Add the prawns and toss to coat. Cover and chill in the refrigerator for 15 minutes.

2. Meanwhile, cook the noodles according to the packet instructions. Drain and spread out on a clean tea towel to dry. Transfer to a baking tray and shape into a large nest that will fit into a frying pan. Place the baking tray in the freezer for about 20 minutes. Line a plate with paper towels.

3. To cook the noodle nest, pour 5 cm/2 inches of oil into a deep frying pan and heat until very hot. Carefully slide the frozen noodle nest into the hot oil and cook for 1 minute, or until golden brown. Transfer to the prepared plate.

4. Whisk together the stock, ketchup, oyster sauce, soy sauce and chilli paste in a small bowl.

5. Heat 1 tablespoon of the oil in a large, non-stick frying pan over a medium–high heat. Add the prawns and cook, stirring frequently, until opaque and cooked through. Remove the prawns from the pan.

6. In the same pan, heat the remaining tablespoon of oil over a medium–high heat. Add the garlic and ginger and cook, stirring, for about 2 minutes, until very fragrant. Add the sauce mixture and cook until the sauce bubbles and thickens. Return the prawns to the pan along with the spring onions. Cook, stirring, for a further 2 minutes, until the sauce is thick and the prawns are heated through.

7. Transfer the noodle nest to a serving platter and spoon the prawns and sauce into it. Serve immediately, using a spatula to cut the nest into wedges so that each diner gets some crispy noodle along with the prawns.

SALMON WITH SOBA NOODLES & CHARD

SERVES: 4   **PREP TIME: 10 MINS**   **COOK TIME: 20 MINS**

INGREDIENTS

6 garlic cloves, very thinly sliced

4 tbsp water

4 tbsp Chinese rice wine or sake

55 g/2 oz sugar

1 tbsp unsalted butter

juice of 1 lime

2 tsp finely chopped fresh ginger

2 tsp curry powder

¼–½ tsp cayenne pepper

4 tbsp olive oil

4 x 175 g/6 oz salmon fillets

½ tsp pepper

350 g/12 oz soba noodles

1 bunch chard, central stems removed and leaves julienned

10 g/¼ oz chopped fresh coriander

salt

1. Combine the garlic, water, wine, sugar and butter in a small saucepan. Bring to a simmer and cook, stirring frequently, for 6–8 minutes, until the mixture is syrupy. Remove from the heat and stir in the lime juice.

2. Combine the ginger, curry powder, cayenne pepper and 2 tablespoons of the oil. Season the salmon with a pinch of salt and the pepper and brush with the spice mixture.

3. Cook the noodles according to the packet instructions, drain and transfer to a large bowl.

4. Heat 1 tablespoon of the oil in a large frying pan over a medium–high heat. Add the chard and a pinch of salt and cook, stirring frequently, for 2–3 minutes until tender. Transfer the chard to the bowl with the noodles and toss to combine.

5. Heat the remaining oil in the same pan. Cook the fish for 3–4 minutes on each side, until nicely seared on the outside and just barely pink in the centre.

6. Divide the noodles between four bowls, top each with a fish fillet and drizzle the candied garlic syrup over, along with several slices of the candied garlic. Serve immediately, garnished with coriander.

PRAWN NOODLE BOWL

This hearty meal-in-a-bowl is packed with delicious Thai-style flavours.

SERVES: 4   **PREP TIME: 10 MINS**   **COOK TIME: 8-10 MINS**

INGREDIENTS

200 g/7 oz rice noodles
2 tbsp groundnut oil
85 g/3 oz unsalted peanuts
1 bunch of spring onions, diagonally sliced
2 celery sticks, trimmed and diagonally sliced
1 red pepper, deseeded and thinly sliced
1 fresh bird's eye chilli, sliced
1 lemon grass stalk, crushed
400 ml/14 fl oz fish stock or chicken stock
225 ml/8 fl oz coconut milk
2 tsp Thai fish sauce
350 g/12 oz cooked peeled tiger prawns
3 tbsp chopped fresh coriander, to garnish

1. Prepare the noodles according to the packet instructions. Drain and set aside.

2. Heat a wok over a medium–high heat, then add the oil. Add the peanuts and stir-fry for 1–2 minutes until golden. Remove with a slotted spoon.

3. Add the spring onions, celery and red pepper and stir-fry over a high heat for 1–2 minutes.

4. Add the chilli, lemon grass, stock, coconut milk and fish sauce and bring to the boil. Stir in the prawns, then return to the boil, stirring. Stir in the noodles.

5. Serve immediately, garnished with the coriander and toasted peanuts.

GARLIC UDON NOODLES WITH CRABMEAT

These super garlicky noodles, topped with succulent crabmeat and an unexpected touch of Parmesan cheese, make a fantastic quick dinner or late-night snack.

SERVES: 4　　　**PREP TIME: 5 MINS**　　　**COOK TIME: 10 MINS**

INGREDIENTS

450 g/1 lb fresh udon noodles
85 g/3 oz unsalted butter
6 garlic cloves, finely chopped
6 spring onions, thinly sliced
1 tbsp oyster sauce
1 tbsp soy sauce
1 tbsp sugar
450 g/1 lb canned crabmeat
25 g/1 oz freshly grated Parmesan cheese, to garnish

1. Cook the noodles according to the packet instructions. Drain and set aside.

2. Melt the butter in a saucepan over a medium–high heat. Add the garlic and spring onions and cook, stirring, for 1 minute. Add the oyster sauce, soy sauce and sugar and cook, stirring, for a further minute.

3. Add the noodles and toss to coat well. Remove from the heat and stir in the crabmeat. Serve hot, garnished with Parmesan cheese.

HERO TIPS

You can also use fresh dressed crabmeat in this dish. Use a mixture of both white and dark meat for a richer, fuller flavour.

VEG OUT

RAMEN WITH PAK CHOI & TOFU

This simple but richly flavoured soup makes a quick and satisfying vegetarian meal. Barbecuing the pak choi and tofu adds an intriguing layer of smokiness to the dish.

SERVES: 4

PREP TIME: 10 MINS, PLUS SOAKING

COOK TIME: 40 MINS

INGREDIENTS

350 g/12 oz extra firm tofu, cut into 2.5-cm/1-inch thick slices

15 g/½ oz dried shiitake mushrooms

1.5 litres/2¾ pints vegetable stock

5 tbsp soy sauce

1 tbsp sake or dry white wine

10-cm/4-inch piece fresh ginger, peeled and sliced

4 tbsp rice vinegar

4 tsp sesame oil

350 g/12 oz pak choi, halved or quartered lengthways

1 tbsp clear honey

225 g/8 oz fresh shiitake mushrooms

350 g/12 oz dried ramen noodles (flavouring sachet discarded, if included)

4 spring onions, thinly sliced, to garnish

1. Place the tofu slices in a single layer on a large baking tray lined with a clean tea towel. Top with another clean tea towel. Place a second baking tray on top and weigh it down with heavy dishes or cans of food to squeeze as much moisture from the tofu as possible. Set aside for 30 minutes.

2. Meanwhile, soak the dried mushrooms in hot water for 30 minutes. Drain, reserving the liquid, and slice the mushrooms.

3. Combine the stock, 4 tablespoons of the soy sauce, the sake, mushroom soaking water, ginger, 1 tablespoon of the vinegar and 1 teaspoon of the sesame oil in a medium-sized saucepan. Bring to a simmer over a medium heat. Reduce the heat to low and simmer for about 15 minutes. Remove and discard the ginger slices. Add the reserved soaked mushrooms and simmer for a further 15 minutes, or until the mushrooms are tender.

4. Meanwhile, preheat the barbecue or grill to medium. Place the pak choi in a microwave safe dish, cover and cook in the microwave on high for about 3 minutes. Whisk together the remaining vinegar, the remaining soy sauce, the honey and the remaining sesame oil in a large bowl. Brush the tofu all over with the sauce, then add the pak choi and fresh mushrooms to the bowl and toss to coat well. Place the tofu and vegetables on the barbecue rack and cook for about 2 minutes on each side, until nicely charred and tender. Brush with any remaining sauce. Slice the tofu into 5-cm/2-inch wide strips.

5. Bring the soup back to the boil. Add the noodles and cook, breaking them up with a spoon, for 3 minutes, or until tender. Stir in the spring onions. Serve immediately, topped with the tofu and vegetables.

HOT & SOUR NOODLES WITH TOFU

SERVES: 4 **PREP TIME: 15 MINS** **COOK TIME: 20 MINS**

INGREDIENTS

3 strips lime rind

2 garlic cloves, peeled

2 slices fresh ginger

1 litre/1¾ pints chicken stock

1 tbsp vegetable oil

150 g/5½ oz firm tofu (drained weight), cubed

200 g/7 oz dried fine egg noodles

100 g/3½ oz shiitake mushrooms, sliced

1 fresh red chilli, deseeded and sliced

4 spring onions, sliced

1 tsp soy sauce

juice of 1 lime

1 tsp Chinese rice wine

1 tsp sesame oil

chopped fresh coriander, to garnish

1. Put the lime rind, garlic and ginger into a large saucepan with the stock and bring to the boil. Reduce the heat and simmer for 5 minutes. Remove the lime rind, garlic and ginger with a slotted spoon and discard.

2. Meanwhile, heat the vegetable oil in a large frying pan over a high heat, add the tofu and cook, turning frequently, until golden. Remove from the pan and drain on kitchen paper.

3. Add the noodles, mushrooms and chilli to the stock and simmer for 3 minutes. Add the tofu, spring onions, soy sauce, lime juice, rice wine and sesame oil and briefly heat through.

4. Divide between 4 warmed bowls, scatter over the coriander and serve immediately.

MUSHROOM & TOFU LAKSA WITH NOODLES

SERVES: 4   **PREP TIME: 15 MINS**   **COOK TIME: 10 MINS**

INGREDIENTS

850 ml/1½ pints vegetable stock

400 g/14 oz canned coconut milk

250 g/9 oz shiitake mushrooms, stalks removed, thinly sliced

150 g/5½ oz firm tofu, cubed

2 tbsp tomato purée

175 g/6 oz fine egg noodles

salt and pepper

8 spring onions, sliced, and 4 tbsp shredded mint leaves, to garnish

SPICE PASTE

2 red chillies, deseeded and chopped

4-cm/1½-inch piece fresh ginger, chopped

2 large garlic cloves, chopped

2 lemon grass stalks, tough outer layers discarded, inner stalks chopped

1 tsp coriander seeds, crushed

6 macadamia nuts, chopped

small handful of coriander leaves

3 tbsp vegetable oil

1. Place the spice paste ingredients into a food processor or blender and process until smooth.

2. Heat a wok over a medium–high heat, add the spice paste and stir-fry for 30 seconds. Pour in the stock and coconut milk, and bring to the boil. Add the mushrooms, tofu and tomato purée and season with salt and pepper. Simmer gently for 5 minutes.

3. Cook the noodles according to the packet instructions.

4. Divide between warmed soup bowls and ladle the spicy tofu broth over. Serve immediately, garnished with spring onions and mint leaves.

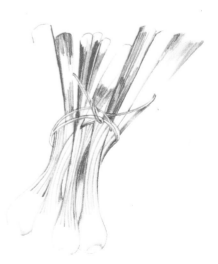

SOBA NOODLE SALAD

A Japanese-inspired salad made with just-cooked soba noodles tossed in a tamari and ginger dressing and speckled with nutrient-boosting broccoli and protein-packed edamame beans.

SERVES: 4   **PREP TIME: 15 MINS**   **COOK TIME: 10 MINS**

INGREDIENTS

150 g/5½ oz soba noodles

200 g/7 oz frozen edamame beans

225 g/8 oz broccoli, cut into small florets, stems thinly sliced

1 red pepper, halved, deseeded and thinly sliced

1 purple or orange pepper, halved, deseeded and thinly sliced

115 g/4 oz chestnut mushrooms, thinly sliced

85 g/3 oz ready-to-eat sprouting sunflower seeds

DRESSING

2 tbsp rice vinegar

2 tbsp tamari (Japanese soy sauce)

4 tbsp rice bran oil

4-cm/1½-inch piece of fresh ginger, peeled and finely grated

1. Put cold water in the base of a steamer, bring to the boil, then add the noodles and frozen edamame beans and bring back to the boil. Put the broccoli in the top of the steamer, then put it on the steamer base, cover and steam for 3–5 minutes, or until the noodles and vegetables are just tender. Drain and rinse the noodles and edamame beans, then drain again and tip into a salad bowl. Add the broccoli, then leave to cool.

2. To make the dressing, put the vinegar, tamari, oil and ginger in a jam jar, screw on the lid and shake well. Drizzle over the salad and toss gently together.

3. Add the red and purple peppers and mushrooms to the salad and toss again. Spoon into bowls, then top with the sprouting seeds and serve immediately.

RAMEN IT HOME!
(THE HEALTH BENEFITS OF NOODLES)

Noodles are a staple part of the diet in many cultures across the world. They are naturally low in fat and a good source of starchy carbohydrate and the whole-wheat versions are rich in dietary fibre. Since noodles tend to contain added salt, there's no need to add salt to the cooking water.

One of the biggest benefits of eating noodles apart from their speed to cook is their ability to easily take on other flavours making them the perfect store cupboard ingredient.

They can form the basis of a substantial meal that's ready in minutes and pair with other food groups perfectly, from fish, meat, chicken or vegetarian meat alternatives such as tofu.

Soba

Soba which are made from pure buckwheat (check the packaging for exact content as it varies) are ideal for those intolerant and avoiding wheat and gluten. The buckwheat used in soba noodles contains about 12–15% protein including the essential amino acid lysine, which isn't present in most cereal grains. It also contains lipids, iron, phosphorous, copper and vitamins B1 and B2.

Choline, another important micronutrient found in buckwheat, plays an important role in our metabolism, particularly regulating blood pressure and liver function.

Udon

Carbohydrate makes up the major nutrient found in udon and it's this which converts to glucose and glycogen in the body. Glycogen becomes both a physical and mental energy source. Compared to other foods such as pasta, udon is digested very quickly and rapidly becomes a source of energy for our mind and body. Udon can possibly aid increased performance when concentration is needed. It might be said that it's well suited for lunch as a healthy afternoon energy source.

Tests have shown that udon is digested at three times the speed of beef making it especially suitable for people who have colds and or weakened digestive function.

Rice

Rice noodles made from white rice flour are a great alternative to those made from wheat and perfect for those avoiding wheat and gluten due to sensitivity or coeliac disease.

Rice noodles are a good source of phosphorus which is the second most abundant mineral in the body. Phosphorus is responsible for strengthening bones and teeth and also assists in filtering out waste in the kidneys, as well as helping the body store, process and use energy.

Egg

As well as being a good source of medium density carbohydrates, these noodles contain similar levels of protein to whole eggs, due to the egg content.

SOBA NOODLES WITH A HONEY-SOY DRESSING

This simple salad, made with fresh soya beans, would be a lovely light meal on a warm evening or a great dish for a picnic.

SERVES: 4   **PREP TIME: 10 MINS**   **COOK TIME: 10 MINS**

INGREDIENTS

225 g/8 oz dried soba noodles

185 g/6½ oz cabbage, shredded

2 carrots, shredded

185 g/6½ oz soya beans, shelled and blanched

4 spring onions, thinly sliced

2 tbsp toasted sesame seeds, to garnish

DRESSING

3 tbsp reduced-salt soy sauce

2 tbsp rice wine vinegar

1 tbsp honey

1 tsp sesame oil

1. Cook the noodles according to the packet instructions. Drain, rinse well with cold water and set aside to cool completely.

2. To make the dressing, whisk together the soy sauce, vinegar, honey and oil in a small bowl.

3. Combine the noodles, cabbage, carrots, beans and spring onions in a large bowl and toss to mix well. Add the dressing and toss again to combine. Serve immediately, garnished with toasted sesame seeds.

HERO TIPS

This delicious and hearty salad will keep well for up to 3 days in the refrigerator.

TEMPEH NOODLE BOWL

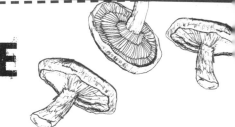

Tempeh has an even higher protein content than tofu and is naturally cholesterol free.

SERVES: 4　　　　**PREP TIME: 10 MINS**　　　　**COOK TIME: 7-10 MINS**

INGREDIENTS

125 g/4½ oz shiitake mushrooms

35 g/1¼ oz miso paste

600 ml/1 pint boiling water

175 g/6 oz mangetout, halved diagonally

200 g/7 oz tempeh or smoked tofu, cubed

1 bunch spring onions, sliced

175 g/6 oz dried udon or soba noodles

1. Remove the stems from the mushrooms and cut a deep cross in the top of the caps.

2. Place the miso and water in a large saucepan and stir thoroughly to dissolve the miso. Place the pan over a high heat and bring back to the boil. Add the mushrooms and mangetout and cook for 2–3 minutes to soften. Stir the tempeh and spring onions into the pan and cook for another 2 minutes.

3. Meanwhile, cook the noodles according to the packet instructions, then divide between warmed bowls.

4. Spoon the tempeh and vegetable mixture over the noodles and serve immediately.

HERO TIPS

To clean your shiitake mushrooms, simply wipe over with a damp piece of kitchen paper. Washing mushrooms exposes them to too much water and can leave them soggy and unappetizing.

NOODLE STIR-FRY

This recipe is fantastically quick, easy and simple, making it an ideal choice when you have little time on your hands but still want a delicious meal.

SERVES: 2   **PREP TIME: 10 MINS**   **COOK TIME: 10 MINS**

INGREDIENTS

140 g/5 oz flat rice noodles
3 tbsp soy sauce
2 tbsp lemon juice
1 tsp granulated sugar
½ tsp cornflour
1 tbsp vegetable oil
2 tsp grated fresh ginger
2 garlic cloves, chopped
4–5 spring onions, trimmed and sliced
2 tbsp rice wine or dry sherry
200 g/7 oz canned water chestnuts, drained and sliced

1. Prepare the noodles according to the packet instructions. Drain and set aside.

2. Mix together the soy sauce, lemon juice, sugar and cornflour in a small bowl. Set aside.

3. Heat a wok over a medium–high heat, then add the oil. Add the ginger and garlic and stir-fry for 1 minute. Add the spring onions and stir-fry for 3 minutes.

4. Add the rice wine, then add the soy sauce mixture and cook for 1 minute.

5. Stir in the water chestnuts and noodles and cook for a further 1–2 minutes, or until heated through. Serve immediately.

RAMEN NOODLE CAKES WITH CURRY & VEGETABLES

A handful of ingredients turn a packet of ramen noodles into a quick, satisfying dinner or a scrumptious late-night snack. This is delicious served with cucumber raita or chutney.

SERVES: 4　　　　**PREP TIME: 5 MINS**　　　　**COOK TIME: 10 MINS**

INGREDIENTS

175 g/6 oz dried ramen noodles (flavouring sachet discarded, if included)
4 eggs, lightly beaten
200 g/7 oz cabbage, shredded
1 large carrot, shredded
4 spring onions, thinly sliced
125 ml/4 fl oz Tikka Masala curry paste
30 g/1 oz plain flour
1–2 tbsp vegetable oil

1. Cook the noodles according to the packet instructions for about 2 minutes. Drain, rinse with cold water and drain well, again.

2. Combine the eggs, cabbage, carrot, spring onions, curry paste and flour in a large bowl and mix well. Add the drained noodles and stir to combine.

3. Heat the oil in a large frying pan over a medium–high heat. Add the noodle mixture, 4 tablespoons at a time. Use the back of a ladle or spoon to flatten each pancake as you add it to the pan. Cook for about 2 minutes on each side until nicely browned and beginning to crisp. Serve hot.

HERO TIPS

Quick-cooking ramen noodles make this recipe lightning fast to make, but any noodles could be substituted successfully.

SICHUAN NOODLES

SERVES: 4   **PREP TIME: 10 MINS**   **COOK TIME: 8-10 MINS**

INGREDIENTS

250 g/9 oz thick egg noodles

2 tbsp peanut or corn oil

2 large garlic cloves, very finely chopped

1 large red onion, cut in half and thinly sliced

125 ml/4 fl oz vegetable stock or water

2 tbsp bottled chilli bean sauce

2 tbsp Chinese sesame paste

1 tbsp dried Sichuan peppercorns, roasted and ground

1 tsp light soy sauce

2 small pak choi or other Chinese cabbage, cut into quarters

1 large carrot, grated

1. Prepare the noodles according to the packet instructions. Drain and set aside.

2. Heat a wok over a high heat and add the oil. Add the garlic and onion and stir-fry for 1 minute.

3. Add the vegetable stock, chilli bean sauce, sesame paste, ground Sichuan peppercorns and soy sauce and bring to the boil, stirring to blend the ingredients together.

4. Add the pak choi quarters and grated carrot and continue to stir-fry for 1–2 minutes, until they are just wilted. Add the noodles and continue stir-frying.

5. Using 2 forks, mix all the ingredients together until the noodles are hot. Transfer to bowls and serve immediately.

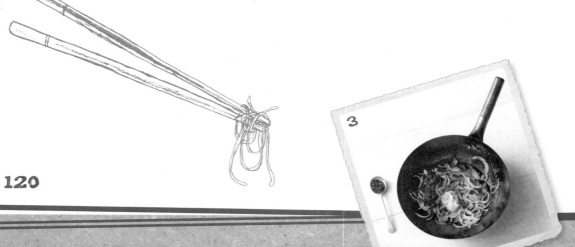

SPICY VEGETABLE & TOFU UDON NOODLES

This is one of those magical dishes where a few simple ingredients transform themselves into a delectable meal in minutes.

SERVES: 4　　　　**PREP TIME: 5 MINS**　　　　**COOK TIME: 15 MINS**

INGREDIENTS

225 g/8 oz French beans, topped and tailed and cut into 2.5-cm/1-inch pieces

2 tbsp water

2 tbsp sriracha

2 tbsp rice vinegar

2 tbsp soy sauce

350 g/12 oz dried udon noodles

1 tbsp vegetable oil

1 tbsp sesame oil

2½ garlic cloves, finely chopped

225 g/8 oz extra firm tofu, cut into 2.5-cm/1-inch cubes

225 g/8 oz baby spinach

2 tbsp toasted sesame seeds, to garnish

1. Place the beans in a microwave-safe bowl with the water. Cover and microwave on high for 2 minutes, then drain.

2. Stir together the sriracha, vinegar and soy sauce in a small bowl.

3. Cook the noodles according to the packet instructions. Drain and set aside.

4. Meanwhile, heat the vegetable oil and sesame oil in a large frying pan over a medium–high heat. Add the garlic and cook, stirring, for 1 minute. Add the tofu and beans and cook, stirring occasionally, for 1 minute, until the beans are tender and the tofu is beginning to brown. Stir in the spinach and cook for 2 minutes, until it wilts. Add the noodles and sauce mixture and toss to combine well.

5. Serve immediately, garnished with toasted sesame seeds.

CRISPY NOODLES WITH PAK CHOI IN OYSTER SAUCE

Lightly cooked pak choi and deep-fried crunchy noodles are a simple but stylish combination.

SERVES: 4 **PREP TIME: 10 MINS** **COOK TIME: 8-10 MINS**

INGREDIENTS

2 tbsp peanut oil, plus extra for deep-frying

100 g/3½ oz dried rice vermicelli noodles

1 tbsp crushed palm sugar or muscovado sugar

1 tbsp rice vinegar

1 tbsp fish sauce

1 tbsp lime juice

6 spring onions, sliced

1 garlic clove, thinly sliced

350 g/12 oz small pak choi, quartered lengthways

3 tbsp oyster sauce

sesame seeds, to sprinkle

1. Heat enough oil for deep-frying in a large saucepan to 180–190°C/350–375°F, or until a cube of bread browns in 30 seconds. Add the noodles in batches and fry for 15–20 seconds, until puffed and golden. Drain on kitchen paper.

2. Heat the sugar, vinegar, fish sauce and lime juice in a small pan, until the sugar dissolves. Boil for 20–30 seconds until syrupy.

3. Heat 2 tablespoons of the oil in a wok and stir-fry the spring onions and garlic for 1 minute. Add the pak choi and stir-fry for 2–3 minutes. Stir in the oyster sauce.

4. Toss the noodles with the syrup and the pak choi. Serve the dish immediately, sprinkled with sesame seeds.

UDON NOODLES WITH KALE & MISO

This simple, nutritious and filling dish is comfort food at its best. Add some grilled tofu for added protein, if you like.

SERVES: 4   **PREP TIME: 10 MINS**   **COOK TIME: 25 MINS**

INGREDIENTS

2 tbsp olive oil

1 large red onion, halved and thinly sliced

½ tsp salt

1 tbsp Chinese black rice vinegar or balsamic vinegar

350 g/12 oz dried udon noodles

2 garlic cloves, finely chopped

350 g/12 oz kale

2 tbsp white miso paste

4 tbsp Chinese rice wine or mirin

4 tbsp water

2 tbsp rice vinegar

1 tbsp unsalted butter

2 tbsp toasted sesame seeds, to garnish

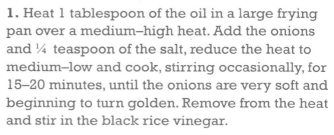

1. Heat 1 tablespoon of the oil in a large frying pan over a medium–high heat. Add the onions and ¼ teaspoon of the salt, reduce the heat to medium–low and cook, stirring occasionally, for 15–20 minutes, until the onions are very soft and beginning to turn golden. Remove from the heat and stir in the black rice vinegar.

2. Meanwhile, cook the noodles according to the packet instructions. Drain and transfer to a large bowl.

3. Transfer the cooked onions to a bowl. Add the remaining oil to the pan and heat over a medium–high heat. Add the garlic and cook, stirring, for 1 minute. Add the kale with the remaining salt and cook, stirring frequently, for 4 minutes, until wilted. Remove from the heat.

4. Combine the miso paste, wine, water and rice vinegar in a small saucepan and bring to the boil over a medium–high heat, stirring constantly until the miso is fully incorporated. Reduce the heat to medium–low and simmer for 2–3 minutes, until the sauce thickens. Remove from the heat and immediately stir in the butter until it is completely melted. Add the sauce to the noodles and toss well.

5. Serve the noodles in small bowls. Arrange some of the kale in a pile on top, with a pile of the onions alongside. Garnish with the sesame seeds and serve immediately.

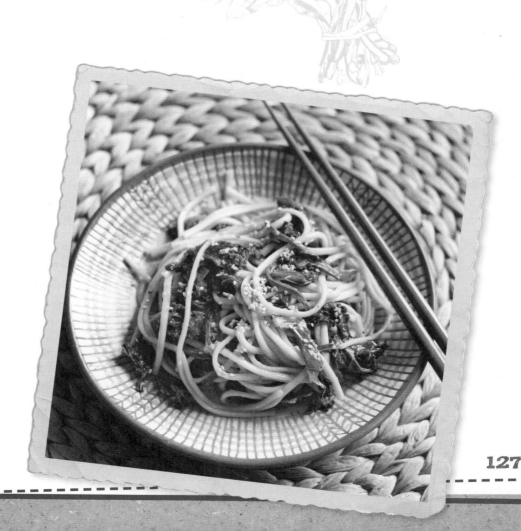

Index